Your Soul Purpose: Reincarnation and the Spectrum of Consciousness in Human Evolution

Dan Desmarques

Published by 22 Lions Bookstore, 2019.

Table of Contents

Copyright Page 1

About the Publisher 3

Introduction 5

The Importance of Reincarnation in Evolution 7

How Do We Evolve? 9

How Imagination Interferes in Evolution 11

The Stages of Change 13

What is the Cause of Human Degradation? 17

What is the Relevance of Suffering in Evolution? 21

The Implications of Reincarnation in Individualism 25

Evolution Beyond Human DNA 27

How Morality Leads to Enlightenment 29

Responsibility as the Basis for Consciousness 31

How to Overcome the Evil of Others 33

How Many Levels Does Consciousness Have? 35

How Evil Interferes With Consciousness? 39

The Illusion of Spiritual Immunity 41

The Path of the Chosen by God 43

The Perception of Justice and the Spiritual Levels 45

How Negative Actions Affect Consciousness 47

The Assimilation of Sin and Divine Punishment 51

A The Bridge Between the Visible and the Invisible 53

How to Awaken Knowledge From Previous Lives?.. 57

The Transmutation of the Identity.. 59

Copyright Page

Your Soul Purpose: Reincarnation and the Spectrum of Consciousness in Human Evolution

By Dan Desmarques

Copyright © Dan Desmarques, 2019 (1st Ed.). All Rights Reserved.

Published by 22 Lions Bookstore and Publishing House

About the Publisher

About the 22 Lions Bookstore:

www.22Lions.com

Facebook.com/22Lions

Twitter.com/22lionsbookshop

Instagram.com/22lionsbookshop

Pinterest.com/22lionsbookshop

Introduction

The human evolution is affected by a multitude of elements, many of which manifest during the process of reincarnation through many lifetimes. Along these paths, even though prosperity tends to seem the prevalent rule that guides everyone towards certain choices in their existence, either more positive or negative, there are many others that tend to be invisible to the masses. These rules are related to karma, sacred geometry and cosmic values. And the distinction between them and our own consciousness, determines our level of success, in our relationships, finances and measurement of happiness. One can't simply be happy without fulfilling his spiritual role in the universe while obeying it. And yet, many people forget this basic principle, namely, when they pursue illusions that don't fulfill them. In this sense, the purpose of this book consists in clarifying the goal of human life and what needs to be taken into consideration to understand how to live it to the fullest within a larger plan, even cosmic, and not simply the one present on planet earth.

The Importance of Reincarnation in Evolution

Reincarnation can drastically alter the condition in which a person develops, but only up to a certain level, since all human beings are endowed with the freedom to think and exercise their imaginative capacity to attract responses that lead them to the universe of their desired experiences. And these are the ones who possess all the potential to alter the planetary state also through an intervention in the present state of global consciousness. From this state of mind, it is possible to enjoy an evolution even higher than this, which should be a permanent ambition of all beings who aspire to enlightenment. For the reverse manifests itself in the many others who regress to lower planes, where the limitations are greater.

To understand these differences, it suffices to observe the very manifestations that life offers us and to correlate the variables with the causes behind all the events that arise. In short, the difference between rich and poor societies within the same planet manifests tendencies of group consciousness on a larger scale. And so, they show us that opportunities and experiences are very different; Levels and learning speeds are unequal; The degree of suffering and happiness are tremendously different. And in this sense, it is so important to recognize why we reincarnate in such nations, as it is to recognize the potential that we have, as spiritual beings, to cross them and choose in which we intend to live. In this context, it is interesting to observe so many people, coming from more developed countries, doing volunteer work, helping or simply living in countries that are very poor. This process of voluntary spiritual regression also occurs between planets, so we should not consider all beings in this situation as fallen angels or punished aliens. Most of the cases, such as those we observe on earth, with indigo children, are volunteers.

The relationship between all beings on the same planet is far more tenuous than one might think, and even the 7 billion people on this planet cannot remove the closeness that exists between all of them, in any corner of the world, and despite the inequalities of the past planetary or interplanetary systems that may seem to separate them.

We are all united, whether we realize this or not, by the same value system. The independent will is not separated from such a system. And karma is just the word we give to the process of ignoring the cosmic rules that govern each of our lives. In fact, the less spiritual and less conscious a person is, the more subject such person is to the karmic consequences of his actions.

This karmic system would not have as much impact if telepathy was an involuntary rather than voluntary phenomenon. For we would automatically perceive the value of empathy, compassion, truth, and cooperation. If we know how, and are sufficiently evolved to do so, the thought of any human being anywhere in the world can be visualized and understood by one elsewhere. For the truth is that most of the thoughts that occupy the mind rarely belong to us, and in some cases they do not even originate in this galaxy or physical plane of reality.

It is because we all share the same collective consciousness, at a subconscious level for the vast majority, that telling a lie is always a spiritual crime against the ones we share it with as much as ourselves and the whole of humanity. Those who lie commit a spiritual sin and do have karmic consequences being attracted to them. As a matter of fact, as a human being evolves to higher states of awareness, he comes to the realization that telling a lie, especially the ones which protect his reputation, contradicts his own spiritual purpose and evolution. And so, he finds himself unable to be amongst those who, by not being tolerant towards differences, for being uninvolved, force one to lie. And sadly, he comes also to the realization that this is a fact within all congregations, as much as it is in the lowest stratums of society, for a tribalistic mindset always invites ignorance in different forms.

Upon this realization, he comes to the conclusion that he cannot share the same space with most humans without causing inevitable conflict and discrimination, starting with a collection of various insults, and ending in violence, and, in some cases, even death. And what a shame it is, when in the name of a lie, crowds sacrifice the best amongst them, when the opposite should be happening, as has always been the desire of God — protect the very few from the many.

How Do We Evolve?

The way in which matter moves on each planet obeys different laws, but all of them are governed by the same order superior to all. Such laws are recognized through spiritual potential. An increasing intention composed by actions in the physical, mental and spiritual plane, lead to the recognition of this same potential. By intention on a physical plane, all actions and decisions are understood; At the mental level, we are talking about the wisdom accumulated through the acquisition of empirical knowledge; as far as spirituality is concerned, we are not necessarily referring to meditation, but all actions that connect the heart with the imagination, thus awakening our spiritual potential. For the opposite of self-destruction through fear and resentment is manifest ambition in the dream composed of emotions, the same state of expectation that a child feels when he looks at the Christmas toys, still wrapped in gleaming paper.

As an example, our spirit can recognize itself in the possibility of flying. We can dream that we can fly and in the dream we fly, even though our physical body cannot fly. And yet the body is material and the spirit is not, so it is the spirit that recognizes the divine laws. If the spirit believes that it can fly, it flies, although it cannot control the body in that sense. It is because of this dream that airplanes, parachutes, hang-gliders, and so many other methods that allow us to hold the body in the air for long periods of time have been created. On the other hand, being spirit separated from the body, we know that in other realities that obey different laws of physics, the spirit can make the body fly, although in the terrestrial reality it can't. Although in this case we have to use matter to make the body fly, as in the case of aircraft construction, in other existential planes, other planets, we can merely use intention.

This does not mean, however, that it is not possible to fly using only mental power on the earth plane. But the physical composition of the planet is such that this power can only be exercised when complemented with a genetic component at the same level. In other words, there is a correlation between our mental and genetic state that needs to be in balance, so that evolution on a spiritual level can benefit both.

An often overlooked but extremely important example to explain this phenomenon can be seen in children equipped with computer programming skills. In general, they are born in families that already have the genes necessary to facilitate this mental exercise. And, even tough it is not possible to state that genes limit development, development itself is not possible without the genes evolving as well. And one of the biggest fallacies yet to be discovered, to the detriment of the billions of dollars made every year by the pharmaceutical companies, benefiting from the ignorance of many, is that we do indeed possess the potential to alter our genetic code. We can do this in three ways, the easiest one being physical, i.e., through food. That is why members of the Rosicrucian school and the Ancient School of Pythagoras have always been vegetarians. It is not possible to evolve rapidly on a spiritual level without a direct intervention in the state of our body through what we ingest. On the other hand, many people destroy the energetic field of their body through irresponsible sex with strangers, and sex with too many partners throughout a lifetime. And this, not only is harmful to the magnetic field of the being, but also to health — mental and physical. The promiscuous tend to suffer more from cysts, ulcers, depression and other organic and mental disorders, which are not as common as the actions behind their emergence.

How Imagination Interferes in Evolution

It is not for the human beings of planet earth to learn to levitate or to fly like their superheroes, the fruit of an imaginary conceived from realities that exist in parallel worlds. It is a waste of time to waste the spirit on tasks that do not develop the soul. And it obeys the rules of development of the planet in which it is inserted. In this sense, the function of beings on planet earth is to learn according to their mind, intelligence, through the relationship with the heart. But many people forget this, when they let themselves be guided by their illogical instincts, or their conscious need to manifest ideas that exist only in the mind, but do not fulfill them or lead to a happy state.

For beings residing on earth, learning refers to the use of intelligence to learn to control matter and thus learn about its laws, although many choose to be controlled by technology, the opinions of others and the state of the planet. Very few can recognize opportunities during times of crisis. During many times of economic crisis, several banking institutions lent money without any conditions or expectations. Few people have noticed it. Among them, many missed the opportunity for thinking that they could never pay such a value back. They were unaware of the fact that they would most likely never have to pay it. Still less considered that during one of these times they can find the ideal moment to apply for a loan and travel to another country where they can live better.

The opposite pole also manifests itself in these cases, when people who have saved a lifetime in richer countries lose everything in a single day. And yet those who allow themselves to be tormented by such events do not verify the opposite reality. Many millionaires arose during major economic crises. Many people have lost their homes during these times, while others have been able to purchase the house of their dreams for up to ten times less than the normal price.

Those who realize enough about the opportunities and possibilities of the material world, understanding all the laws involved in it, become capable of ascending to other planes of reality where they continue to apply the same prior principles, now in a more generalized and subtle materiality, such as in the control of a business or businesses. At a higher level, we would say with the power of the mind. But the truth is that on a planet where the value of every human being is still measured by how much money he can get, spiritual evolution must necessarily cross this quadrant of reality. Only then can one really change the world and be an altruistic philanthropist. A poor man cannot help anyone. His power is extremely limited. And therefore, his intelligence and spiritual state, are also limited, although we can consider such a situation as a "dormant potential."

Each planet assumes a generalized purpose, but in all of them there are laws that coordinate the sacred geometry in the same sense. In the case of planet earth, this concerns learning to use matter to understand the spirit and thus ascend spiritually. The beings who are on this path should dedicate themselves to experiencing life as much as possible — through work and constant learning, accompanied by feelings, the same feelings that provide consciousness with the sensation of right and wrong. And the fastest route to this is through permanent contact with other cultures and different ways of life.

All beings who fail in this learning suffer consequences at the level of the physical body and move quickly to death, while those who succeed learn more about themselves and transform their existential dynamics more quickly, achieving their dreams and dreaming afterwards even more and successively in the path of developing spiritually.

Spiritual evolution is so much about the imaginary that the distinction between a guru and a schizophrenic is not always clear. While this is so, many seek shortcuts in the field of psychotropic drugs, which, with few exceptions, allow few distinctions between a shaman and a mere addict of chemical pleasures. Yet, while many spiritualists and enlightened ones may be mistaken for madmen, the fact remains that "truth is not for all men but only for those who seek it" (Ayn Rand).

The Stages of Change

The desire of a human being can be analyzed in terms of levels of mental maturity, and spiritual maturity, although both are related, and materiality, or rather potential, in relation to the material reality at his disposal.

Although the vast majority of people are concentrated in the material component, it depends entirely on the other two to justify the validity and value of a desire. Only then can visualizations, referring to the particularities of these three areas, transfer the individuality to a higher plane. In fact, depression, nightmares, and fears are, in most situations, only outward representations of a negative, downward, and sickly inner state. The person who suffers is sick, but only because he is not progressing. And any therapy that does not reshape a person's ability to evolve will never be effective, nor will it produce results that can be measured in the long run.

That said, the most elemental dream is that which respects material and social illusions, such as having money, success, and fame. It is elementary because it is related to illusions aroused from needs, which fundamentally reflect, emotional pain. In a higher level than this, although basic, we have the materiality itself, the necessity combined with the act, motivated by ambition. It is the getting a car, a house, a job, and even friends and sexual partners, a marriage, children, etc.

Above this materialistic state, but relevant to know the higher stages of the soul, we find the need for change, for transformation. And it is not by chance that people who strive to evolve suffer more from change. The suffering arises only because they consider the two realities, inner and outer, different. And their suffering is no more than a lack of awareness for the need to take responsibility for those who have a much lower level of responsibility. Thus, a high dream would have to be, not only altruistic, but also egoistic, at an equal level. Here we find the relevance of connecting the ever-changing elements of life, even if such changes are, or seem, too fast.

The secret to success on this plane lies in happiness, in focusing on the divine spark that is latent in our hearts. Only in this way can we desire and embrace change, in total awareness of permanent happiness, as well as the negative elements that are disassociated from us, being them thoughts, physical elements, or even people.

The spiritual dream through the imagination represents a search for inner transformation, focusing on the attainment of the satisfaction of feelings — the pursuit of happiness and, ultimately, peace of mind. To this extent, we know that in the greatest material chaos we find the least dynamic earth potential and in the most peaceful organization the greatest potential. Still, any meaningful transformation has to emerge from chaos, and chaos is always the way the inner revolution manifests itself. A human does not transform until he suffers first. And although suffering is not necessary, any detachment causes it, especially when this detachment represents the things or people we love the most. Thus, the being that controls matter better, more quickly rises spiritually, being the one who suffers most in this alchemical process. And that is why understanding alchemy is relevant, not only to understand the dynamics of reality in which we live, but also those that we awaken inwardly.

We know that matter is controlled by energy, and so we also know that less spiritual beings believe that it can only be controlled by other materializations, such as money, knowledge and social opportunities. They are slaves to the outer universe. And any person who identifies himself as the victim of fate or fortune in general is necessarily a slave to the reality in which he enters, regardless of his lifestyle and the illusion of freedom he can feel or convey to others. The truth is, a car, a family, a house, and vacations, two to three times a year, do not make a person happy and are not significant to represent freedom. However, because people believe this, these are the limits of their ambition. And if they dedicate a whole existence to these ends, they consider themselves happy, even if they do not reach them.

It is not surprising, therefore, that in a later reincarnation they must reincarnate like a pig or a sheep, and await a whole existence for their carnage. For only in this way can they understand what they did not understand before. And what is death, but an even more painful carnage? Many and many souls remain, after their physical death, hovering in the world, suffering for years, and even decades, the reflection of their ignorance. In a way, the afterlife represents the most painful spiritual state for the many ignorant people who experience it. And how strange it is that among all fears this is the most ignored.

I do not believe that hell is worse than this spiritual state. In fact, hell is well represented by the state of planet earth. The pain of accelerated awareness, on the other hand, contains a thousand times more suffering; a suffering so intense, that those who become mad in the process, are the demons known.

This spiritual state can only be calmed through spiritual possession. And it is for this reason that the more atheists there are in the world, and the more ignorant human beings are in relation to their spiritual state and the mechanics of existence of which they are part, the more living beings are tormented by spiritual entities. And interestingly, the most tormented are non-believers, atheists, as well as those addicted to drugs, alcohol, and other narcotic substances. And isn't even more interesting to verify that they tend to be the same? It is truly extraordinary to see the downward spiral in which many human beings meet, for with every step they take toward lower levels of their inferno, more predictable they become.

We can neglect demonic power, when we, as a species, are largely destroying ourselves. It all begins with the first vice, the first laugh at the spiritual themes, the first insult to a Christian, Hindu or Gnostic. From there, the idiots are signaled, and the tormented souls know who to look for, and how to satisfy the needs they had in life, through the living. And how interesting it is that so many people think thoughts are impossible to control, for the only thoughts you cannot control are the thoughts that do not belong to you.

The spiritual and physical world have never been so united, and humankind has never been so numb and has never been so ignorant, on such a large scale, in its history. Therefore, an apocalyptic destruction, in this case, is not only logical, but necessary. The question we must ask is: Is this the solution?

The reason I raise this question is simple. All the religions of the planet are corrupted, and the number of those chosen for salvation is so small that they could hardly rebuild an entire planet by themselves. Being adopted by more loving alien races than the human race would make much more sense, in fact. And from a spiritual point of view, only this would allow a higher manifestation after such destruction.

What is the Cause of Human Degradation?

Most people nourish, through degrading attitudes, an egocentric greed, which makes their existences very limited and vulnerable to the effects of the spiritual world. So quickly do they enrich themselves, as soon as they die with a drastic illness or a fatal accident. And this fact explains why, in poorer societies, the population believes in both luck and divine will, in total apathy to their own responsibility over their lives. In fact, when ignorance is tremendous, everything occurring to us seems to be the result of luck or higher powers. It takes a certain intellectual capacity and spiritual maturity to understand the relationship between the physical world and the spiritual world, and religions do not always want people to achieve it. In fact, a modern religion is rarely for this purpose because its record is based on control, and control is not possible without mass acceptance.

It is a fact already known in psychology that the masses are never receptive to the truth. The generally infantile state, and extremely low morale, prevents awareness from manifesting. Moreover, awareness can never manifest without ethics, and ethics depends on a clear understanding of the moral values that must govern mankind. And how can anyone understand morality when their mind is shaped and blinded by the filter of culture and nationalization?

You know, with a sense of strong nationalism, you or someone else will never understand what ethics is. The two mental states, tribalism and individualism, are incompatible. You can't see people as divisions of something imagined, as is the case of nations, or material aspects such as physical appearance and color of the skin, and then say that you are a person with good thoughts, spiritual, or whatever that is in this sense. All people who pride themselves on their nation, but believe they can evolve spiritually, are hypocrites and idiots. How can you be proud of something you have not done, such as being born in a nation, and then want to be proud of something you cannot even understand? No wonder meditation is so difficult for these people. A good book would bring more results than sitting on the floor with their eyes closed, and expect a mind full of stupidity to light up. Can a lamp painted black ever brighten? And what kind of light can a green or red lamp give? A crazy person who meditates, becomes more crazy. A hypocritical person, who meditates, never reaches results. And a selfish person, who meditates, becomes a kind of autistic disguised in social masks.

There is no practical response I can give these people whenever they ask me for help in their meditation practice. I've been hearing the same questions for over 25 years. But the answer, denied by all, is the same: An ignorant mind can never achieve results by ignoring its ignorance. This should be obvious, shouldn't it? And yet many people with college degrees, many psychologists, many psychiatrists, and many scientists I've met, can't understand it.

It does not matter the social status, the educational level, or the financial level that a being owns, for the laws that govern planet earth follow an order that transposes every imaginable situation into these planes. In this sense, we all learn.

An individual can excel in the control of a small material universe and thus acquire a great self-control that allows him to rise spiritually, or be poor in controlling a vast material universe, which will not allow him to evolve with it. In the emotions we feel, in our interaction with the reality plane that life offers us, we will recognize our spiritual state, because it can only be moving towards either greater peace or suffering. And true peace, however, is not possible without true knowledge, self-realization, and the satisfaction of three types of needs: physical, spiritual, and mental.

Many people who seek love, forget the importance of sex in their life. Many people in pursuit of sexual pleasure forget the importance of love in their life. And in both cases we are talking about physical pleasures.

Although getting a luxury car or buying a castle, may for many be a pleasure superior to love or sex, the truth is that, as human beings, we always create priority in what touches us on a more general level. If this were understood, couples would be happier. For all the discussions arise from the mind of unfinished human beings. And psychology can do little or nothing for someone who has no interest in evolving through reading and study, through humility, and through responsibility.

YOUR SOUL PURPOSE

Apologizing is an act, strangely, difficult, if not impossible, for many people. And in this sense, being stupid is not as relevant as realizing stupidity and being able to learn from the consequences of our actions. For when many women complain that men seek only the younger, less sexually experienced, they forget that a life of whoring is not a right but a decision on which they must be responsible. For men are never obliged to accept women who commit prostitution. And although I am not surprised that one day some woman tries to pass a law that makes it impossible for men to reject disgusting women, the truth is that we can't speak of equal rights until we can understand the differences in these equalities. For the truth is that, like whores, such women cannot be good mothers or faithful companions. In each sexual act, a spiritual celebration of a marriage, the brain becomes corrupted by the lack of empathy in the act. And it is precisely the empathy that certifies someone as capable of raising a healthy child.

The world does not need more psychopaths created by mad mothers. And that is why men have the right, not only to reject, but to totally ostracize women with a prostitute's attitude, for the sake of human evolution.

Much could also be said about the men who exist today, but interestingly, women always choose the most promiscuous and aggressive, considering them more appropriate, stimulating, competent and sexually compatible. It remains for us to think about this phenomenon while we consider whether the conclusions are relevant. For what people desire and demand of others is not often what they do in their lives.

What is the Relevance of Suffering in Evolution?

In suffering, matter encounters destruction and, in peace, fusion with the remaining elements. By becoming better acquainted with his spiritual identity, a being is guided by an understanding of the laws that govern the universe and the principle behind all of them, as is the case with the principle behind the sacred geometry of the elements that make up matter. And, in the opposite direction, it is directed towards its destruction, because, in the absence of harmony, the universe destroys what is not compatible with its order in order to be able to maintain it.

A being cannot contradict the laws of the universe, but can act upon them by creating divergences and various original hypotheses from the same pre-existing principle. In short, a human being can create by following the divine law, but can't contradict it. It is present in all elements, and even in the structure of thought and the mind that creates it.

A human being can act as a god and be a god of his world, directing himself to possess more power, but cannot act against the laws of God, for these are superior to him, are in his origin, and are of which he is composed. To act against the higher consciousness would be to act against oneself. Such is the truth that can recognize him at his core, both in pain and deepest happiness.

Suicide of the soul, by silencing the conscience to the truth, is therefore the most sinful act that one can have, though it is the most common. All who commit it, decrease in their spiritual level, moving towards a reality where materiality assumes more and more importance, so that they can learn more, in a simple way, about spirituality. And the greatest simplicity of all in relation to materiality arises when one has no control over it. This is very obvious with extreme poverty, hunger, and disabling diseases.

The deep suffering of the Roman and Medieval Eras did not diminish the degree of spirituality in the world but rather propelled it to higher levels. It now remains for us to know whether another era of global suffering is needed if human beings are to be pushed back into a higher understanding of their spirituality.

While some only learn when on the verge of death, and others not even so, a few regress spiritually before the suffering promoted by the previous ones. Therefore, the future of an entire planet like this must inevitably reside in the relationship between the lesser and the more spiritual, and the wars for the rights of both continue, as they have always been, to be at the center of the discords and conflicts that define a generalized destiny.

On the other hand, taking into consideration that reincarnation spreads humans all over the world, making them reborn as what once was perceived as their enemies or inferior, all wars are nothing but wars against ourselves.

As far as occupied space is concerned, there are no limitations, for a being of any existential dimension can reincarnate in any other dimension of existence. Obviously, there are always present rules that justify the passage from one plane to another. But, these rules are superior to any planetary norm of space and time. Thus, a being can either be ready for a reality of slightly higher level, or another of a much higher level, but will make the passage according to the level reached at the moment of his physical death. So the transition is much easier for those who have been able to live an entire existence naturally and age quietly. Such a transition is always more painful and difficult for those who died abruptly while still young. Nevertheless, this level is measured by the degree of awareness reached.

Consciousness is not without judgment and is not independent of karmic laws. A being who has disengaged himself from his behavior, losing knowledge about the purpose of the spirit, may find himself reincarnating in an environment that further strengthens his awareness, and within the same planet in which he is inserted. He can reincarnate in another reality similar to present time, or in a reality of another time period. But, he can also reincarnate in another planet, if the process of consciousness does not find in this same planetary state a satisfactory situation to the learning that in the meantime has been proven necessary.

Depending on the degree of our consciousness and the learning that the soul lacks to develop it, we can reincarnate immediately after death in another country and in another social situation, more suited to the manifest needs of the spiritual consciousness acquired. Hence there are innumerable cases of Jews reincarnating as Catholics, and Japanese as Americans, or, Americans as Arabs.

However, we can also be transported to a medieval age, or to a distant future, such as a thousand years ahead of our time, where cars fly and society is organized differently. We can also reincarnate in another reality, where beings are not human, but only humanoids, and communicate differently, and have a different skin color; or even on another planet, where people are the same as terrestrials, but live life differently and have mental potentials distinct from those we know.

There are as many possibilities as there are to those our imagination can create, for everything we imagine connects in the universe of possibilities already existing and that our soul recognizes because some spirit connected to us has already manifested itself there.

The planets we can imagine exist and other people may be able to imagine the same without sharing our imagination in co-creation. All the realities we can conceive in our minds exist as well, for there are as many parallel realities as our decisions can form. Just consider that if we can predict the future, we can create the future, and if we can create a future, we should always be able to predict it.

On the other hand, we can't predict what does not already exist, and that is why the illusion of the future is necessary and real in proportion to what we do on a present plane. In fact, elites have always sought to accelerate or maintain a certain reality through the awareness, maintenance and manipulation of the masses. And from there, we can consider that there are as many possible future realities as we can visualize.

The potential of the human mind, containing its focus on creativity, will be able to observe in the dream the whole world of soul possibilities. We may even, by following these premises, say that all present-day human beings, dreaming about the future, may acquire a perfect view of all the future realities existing in parallel in present time. In fact, "the search for truth is more precious than its possession" (Albert Einstein).

The Implications of Reincarnation in Individualism

The consciousness that accompanies reality is not defined by levels comparative to this same reality, since spiritual levels are independent of human conceptions about the quality of reality. The mechanics of spirituality are far more complex than the potential of human thought, and therefore always higher than this. In this sense, a being who needs greater awareness of his individuality and uniqueness may be born in a location in which he feels quite isolated. It may even be a hostile environment, in which he suffers many aggressions from his parents. And yet, the universe is perfect in its harmony and everything has a purpose. Therefore, for every being in similar situations, the purpose will be corresponding to the designs of his soul. For one, it may be the development of his consciousness in the face of his oneness, so that by acquiring greater potential to deal with responsibility for his own existence, he may experience situations he would not otherwise be able to experience, and to another person in a similar reality may be to acquire awareness of the material universe and the simplicity of the cause-effect system, so that he may acquire the responsibility of learning about the humility which is underlying to the harmonious living with a commitment to life itself.

Between two beings in a hostile environment, one can learn about the purpose of life, while another is learning about his or her personal purpose. Hence, two persons who have experienced the same primordial experiences may act quite differently in the life to come and have completely differentiable existences, as well as modes of thinking which are themselves distinct.

For every existence there is a purpose that only finds answer in the soul of each one. Human spirits all assume a distinct individuality, which forms the designs of existence that they promote along their unique development journey, in a joint and global process, which we can call collective consciousness towards the divine purpose.

It should be noted, however, that it is in this intercalation of consciences, that different people come together on the same plane of reality, share experiences and learnings, each assuming the role that corresponds to one, developing, loving and living, in the negative and in the positive, because we both learn from conflict, as we learn in peace, although the latter is more desirable for many. Such is the harmony of existence, in which every moment finds justification in the soul of each being.

Each state of life assumes a purpose appropriated to consciousness, and no reality can be the same for any being. The experience that each individual feels has a unique purpose that only he can interpret because there is a perfect correlation between the consciousness of each soul and the experiences that he experiences and feels at his core. In this cycle of experiences lies a harmony in which we all move, in an infinite perfection of which we are part. This Pythagorean mathematics contains all knowledge, already interpreted or ignored, for no one lives apart from Divine laws, not even atheists.

In each decision we find a new correlation with reality that never ceases to fit into the harmony that this same reality presupposes, between the designs of the spirit, the individual purpose and the material reality. The correlation is permanent, although we have the power to change the contexts in which we acquire the learning, through the possibility of deciding in the course of the experiences that we live. As Mark Twain said, "No wonder the truth is stranger than fiction; fiction has to make sense."

Evolution Beyond Human DNA

There are several possibilities in the universe of parallel realities, but also in the space-time operating simultaneously with ours, and even worlds, in other galaxies, so we can say that in our material reality different forms of life can manifest. Namely, and especially, those that most easily cross the flows of energy between matter, as is the case of spirits devoid of body. Among them, some correspond to human beings already devoid of a physic, which we recognize as deceased, and others to alien beings of other dimensions and more subtle frequencies.

In fact, NASA currently recognizes about 100 billion Earth-like planets, where life, as here on earth, may exist. This means that if we multiply this 100 billion planets by the possible parallel realities, we get more than a trillion possibilities. And how can a human brain so limited by earthly reality understand this or all the possibilities that such truth encompasses?

Few people have visited all the countries and cultures of the earth. And that alone is a tremendous experience for the soul. So what can we say of people who laugh at the possibility of extraterrestrials existing? Personally, I think we can only feel sadness over the tremendous brain limitation they have. Such brain would probably explode if they saw a UFO. On the other hand, it is scientifically proven, mainly by DNA studies, in addition to several archaeological researches, although not yet widely divulged, that the human being is, in its physical form, a hybrid descendant of several other alien races, which programmed our DNA in order to limit the potential for spirituality. For, unfortunately, the human being was created to be a slave, inferior to those who gave him origin.

The concept of God, which in Hindu culture assumes a far more comprehensive perception than in Western culture, is not sufficient to account for all human development, and religious books contain interpretative limitations that limit the ability of many people to understand great truths. This closely guarded secret is what has allowed the rise of monarchical and priestly elites, who use it to expand and secure their power. For only the understanding of our limitations enables us to secure the transcendence of these, at most, through the control of those who are unaware of theirs.

At the same time, among the many possibilities of existence, it will be more easily manifested in our material plane that which can best be correlated with it. In a more comprehensive way, we speak of all the races of beings that are in the same plane of materiality or that can manifest themselves in this. This is because, interaction with a material universe requires material existence, without which such interaction would not be possible. Hence, much of the physical evolution of the human being makes sense in order to promote attributes relevant to this reality, such as trust, determinism, analytical potential and the capacity for defense. The naive never had a good future. And it was naivety, largely innocent, that led to the extermination of many tribes and civilizations of the past.

That said, we can't speak of evolution or moral values, without correlating these elements with the survival of the individual and his species. This need is present in all elements of the universe, although it is dormant in cases where it has not yet proved necessary. For we do not know what confrontation is until we face an enemy, and forget what is not relevant with relative ease.

Many people think that the dog has always existed and they do not know that it is a human creation from the wolf. And this is a new type of ignorance, as much as many people do not know exactly how the sperm fertilizes the egg and babies are born. It is really extraordinary when a species is unaware of reproduction. And yet, such is the case with a large number of human beings in the present times.

How Morality Leads to Enlightenment

The path of God unites reality and beings from this reality according to principles that develop from the most physical and simple to the most subtle and spiritual. Therefore, the beings most easily manifested in our physical reality are those most directly associated with it by their relation of kinship and physical proximity. We include here all the humanoid beings that populate other planets, but also those that populate this, through different temporal and spatial manifestations.

Because this book does not deal with alien races, we will not focus here on this aspect. Still, it is interesting to note that the greatest technological changes in history have come about thanks to research in the field of ufology and fallen alien ships; as well as note that several of the most influential spiritualists and writers believe they receive their knowledge by interplanetary inspiration.

Despite the choice in methods for ascension, the purpose of existence on earth is to acquire responsibility for our own behavior. It is through the effects of our behaviors that we can best understand the value of life. And yet, these effects can only be in fact understood after traumatic experience and losses. Many people simply cannot understand life without first losing something. It is only through loss that the value of what is lost is truly understood.

Given that behavior is part of a system of cause and effect, we know that all action will provoke a reaction, an impact, which will somehow reflect upon us. When we receive the resulting impact from our action, we may feel guilty or responsible. However, guilt does not allow us to understand the causes of the problem and, to escape this painful and unresolved feeling, people tend to change the original cycle, making the effect a cause of self. That is, they blame those who have been assaulted by their own aggressions and thus make the victim an aggressor who deserved the aggression. And, in general, they try to change the cycle by changing circumstances. And yet, they are always surprised when the cycle of change repeats the same effects, when different protagonists say the same or complain about it. They do not understand what they do wrong.

Despite everything, despite what we can read, we will never understand what we can't accept. And yet, in a general way, all the dynamics of problems can be synthesized in relatively common causes:

- Selfishness or egocentrism;

- Lack of empathy and compassion;

- Lack of responsibility.

It is relatively easy to see how these three elements blend together and can be summarized in one or a few words. But in general, so is reality. The word we are looking for here is awareness. First, awareness of personal rights, but simultaneously, awareness of the rights of others. Also almost simultaneously, the awareness of self-respect, as much as respect for the individuality of other people.

Morality will seem in this context something still very far from the mind, but not so much as empathy is close to the concept of inter-responsibility. For when we understand the other, we understand the dynamics of the whole, regardless of how many individuals are involved.

The relationship in a marriage between a man and a woman is exactly the same between a man and five women, or five men and a woman, if we answer only to the moral component. And that is why when values are shared entirely at the same level, such marriages, or communities, are actually possible. In other words, it is not the act, but the betrayal of our values, the moral aspect of the dynamics on which we orient our existence, which damages our soul and deeply hurts us.

Responsibility as the Basis for Consciousness

The absence of responsibility creates a kind of predisposition that allows the development of the illusion of perfection or idealization of a person and his actions. In other words, it creates a mental system that leads to narcissism. And the narcissist really believes that his actions are innocent, by eliminating guilt through any possible justification. In fact, it is the prevalence of lying, dissimulation, and manipulation of others, in order to justify otherwise reprehensible behaviors that lie behind psychopathic behavior. It is an egocentric cycle that limits consciousness in such a way that not even the words or suffering of others creates any effect on the individual.

In an attitude of illusory integrity, often manifested as arrogance, such person will consider that he is not responsible for negative cycles of action, and will prevent himself from learning from his mistakes. Unable to learn from mistakes, he will not be able to discern successes, and will believe in luck or manipulation of reality to attain happiness.

If we want to measure the potential for success in a person, we can measure the state of their mental health, and the simplest way is to measure the individual's responsibility for his actions and the consequences of them. For when we think that reality has to be manipulated rather than understood, and when we believe that the evils of life arise from accidents, we lose consciousness of something that transposes in a vast way all the illusions that reality, and even our behaviors, can allow viewing. That is, we lose consciousness of the divine purpose in our life. And that is why such people feel so devoid of meaning in their life or purposes. They can even create them briefly, but are unable to follow them.

In fact, people with low levels of responsibility can never be good employees, friends or marriage partners. Their mental state makes them too unpredictable and unable to follow established and agreed plans, or even their promises. When a psychopath promises to improve, he may even believe what he is saying, but is unable to keep his promise. Hence the psychopaths promise more when they are desperate, trapped, and in need of urgent help, and not so much of their own free will.

It is easy to believe in a psychopath, because they really believe what they say, and because they have experience in not being believed, know how to exaggerate their emotional demonstrations. They really know how to make others believe they would never betray in a relationship, or steal personal property, or get personal information in order to manipulate, but that's exactly what they do when the opportunity arises. In fact, their mental state makes them prone to follow suggestions from others, so even the psychopath who has no intentions of stealing is easily convinced of this by another psychopath like him. And psychopathic women who really want to marry and have a stable relationship with someone, betray with tremendous ease, when they find a man as psychotic and manipulative as they are.

We can even say that the greatest punishment a psychopath can get comes from his own friends, since no normal person or with high levels of responsibility, is willing to associate with these individuals. My personal experience has shown me that all psychopaths associate with equally sick people, or too frail and isolated to defend themselves or reject them. That's why psychopaths prefer the elderly, the children, and the sick.

When their greed is higher than that, they opt for professions where they can exercise their psychosis with more freedom. And this is the case for doctors, nurses, psychiatrists, psychologists and politicians. The number of criminals seeking these professions is enormous. And it is really shocking to see a psychopath occupying the position of psychologist and being trusted by people ignorant of their danger. On the other hand, personal experience has shown me that only very sick people in the head believe in what a psychopathic psychologist says.

How to Overcome the Evil of Others

God has a purpose for our lives, which goes beyond actions and events. Hence we sometimes have to be confronted with realities in which we will inevitably err, so that we may learn what will be necessary to the following experiences, and not necessarily to improve our state in the former. In this sense, insanity, like many forms of madness, assumes a direct relation with the moral laws and laws of truth that govern the world. It is impossible to succeed on a personal or financial level without understanding this.

In fact, the same thing happens when someone hurts us and we see no chance to protect ourselves from this evil. For in this case the purpose may be simply the awareness that we have to change our lives and not so much that we have to learn to deal with such people or even insist on an impossible resolution for an inevitable conflict.

It is not necessary for a person to become evil in order to protect himself from evil, but it is necessary for him to know evil, to identify it, to distinguish it, and to learn not only to protect himself against evil, but also to fight against evil. What this person does afterwards with the knowledge and power acquired is a personal decision and not a cause-effect relation. If so, it would be tantamount to saying that all people who learn boxing to defend themselves tend to punch others. The truth is that people who know how to defend tend to best identify danger and have the courage to know how to stop it when they observe it. That is why I believe that a religion without the teaching of combat will always be incomplete. And although this seems ridiculous for many, more ridiculous is what we see today, with the total disbelief and disinterest in knowing evil.

As I have mentioned in many religious groups, the fear of recognizing evil and speaking of it, opens space for evil to infect any group, so anyone who fears evil is vulnerable to it. And so it is, with all the people I knew and feared to speak of evil. Their spirit is infected and corrupted. For fear creates a very weak vibration that favors negative spiritual intervention.

In reality, negative and positive energies are not as opposed in manifestations as they are in mental states, because the negative is always inferior to the positive. In other words, only fear, resentment, hatred and anger can weaken the spirit.

When we speak, therefore, of responsibility as human purpose, we speak of something more encompassing, and which is within the level of consciousness. This consciousness encompasses all plans, not just the intellectual, rational or spiritual. Awareness for inner and outer combat is as relevant as any. Awareness for humility and vulnerability as well. "We know the truth, not only with reason, but also with the heart" (Blaise Pascal).

How Many Levels Does Consciousness Have?

Consciousness can be considered on different levels: At the most elementary levels we have a direct awareness of action, such as "do unto others what you would have done unto you"; At intermediate levels we will be aware of the effects of action. That is, the knowledge of the result of a cycle of attitudes and behaviors; At the highest levels we have the consciousness of the purpose, in which the process, the cause and the effect, interact to give shape to the reality that serves as a vehicle for awareness.

These three levels may be present simultaneously, but it is only the highest level of consciousness that remains unchanged all the time, for in any system of reality the being must be able to understand more about himself through contact with experiences which cover his existence.

In order for this awareness to develop, responsibility must be developed in parallel, because both things are inseparable. But responsibility can't be fully understood without a purpose that justifies it. That is why morality without egotism is rarely a true morality, but only a group morality, or social. It is not surprising, therefore, when we look at stories of people behaving in a certain way in public and in a very different way in private.

The ultimate responsibility manifests itself in the ability to recognize the potential to control the learning exhibited in life experiences. Therefore, a person who is fully responsible is one who can recognize in his victories the ability to make the right decisions and, in his defeats, the mistakes of decisions made. Hardly anyone can understand morality without understanding the opposing poles that comprise it, without understanding that a good can cause evil and evil can cause good.

To illustrate this fact I will give you a personal explanation. In my naiveté, in the past, when I found people who were suffering from their psychoses, I offered them mental health books to help them. The result was that such people would become even better than they were in the art of lying and manipulating others. For by knowing how the brain really works, they have not changed their nature, but have become worse. And what about friends to whom I have offered books to help them with their struggles? They became arrogant, and began to insult me by saying that the person I am and what I write is distinct, as if accusing me of not being the author of what I write. Many, in their envy, began to use my knowledge against me, to try to make me stop writing books. The insults are aimed at my destruction as an author, and this is due to envy. In other cases, people began to speak in public, exposing my knowledge to crowds without ever mentioning the source, and because knowledge does not belong to them, they have confused entire crowds with subjects they do not really understand. These are examples of goods that have become evil.

What about evils that become social goods? I give as an example the case of a psychologist who purposely destroyed a relationship I had, instead of helping the person I sent her, to solve her childhood problems and traumas. The patient spoke of attempts at suicide, promiscuity, drugs she smoked, alcohol abuse, her difficulties in employment, etc. The psychologist ignored all this, and concentrated on destroying the relationship. And this same woman asked me not to attack the psychologist any more, after I had insulted her in public, and also asked me not to write any letters that would make her lose her job. And only a few months later I discovered that my ex-girlfriend's brother's girlfriend was visiting that same psychologist. That is, when we do not exterminate social cancers, they spread and make more people sick. In this case, the ideal would be to make this woman lose her license to practice psychology, and if it was not possible, give her a strong blow.

The idea that an action can be separated from its moral function belongs only to the mind of very ignorant people who do not understand the function of law, order, and justice, and believe in the patriarchal function of the state, as children, whose need to replace parents for any other adults, leads them to forget the implications of justice. And that is why so many injustices are committed in our society. The more people fear to exercise justice by their own hands, the more those who can't be stopped, will carry out criminal acts against society itself.

We must never forget that the first act of any tyrannical government was to remove the arms of its citizens in order to exercise tyranny over them. It is because people assume the social hierarchy is immune to public judgment, that so many fools assume a power they should not have. And this is how the wolves of society, hidden in sheep's clothing, continue to deceive the masses. For, despite everything, the reputation of this psychologist continues spreading, for newspapers, magazines, etc. This psychopath continues to spread her evil through her masks.

One of the facts that many Christians ignore about the history of Christ is that he really understood these opposites. To the people of his time, he was a rebel, opposing the order of the system, opposing extremely popular ideas, and criticizing social values. And yet he was right about what he said. Christ was not afraid of direct confrontation with the authorities, and of exposing them as hypocrites. He lost his life for that. But how often do we not do the same with those who expose the evils of society by ignoring these people as Christ was ignored?

Today's reality is not much different from two thousand years ago. There are still many wolves hiding behind sheep's skin.

The distance between the cause and the consequences of our actions, even when we are passive in life, as is the case with the many sheep of society, can be analyzed in temporal space. And so we can say that it is possible to live a life full of happiness, but not without the responsibility it demands. Knowing how to live in happiness means taking responsibility for the decisions we make in life — being able to learn from mistakes and correcting them when possible. In the ability to look at problems and solve them, we learn their mechanism and the dynamics involved, namely when what we ignore affects us back.

How Evil Interferes With Consciousness?

We can say that evil exists insofar as it is intrinsic to reality. But this reality is not relative. What moves in the direction of the divine is positive and what does not follow along the same path causes pain, being in this context a type of negative.

The positive and the negative are what define good and evil. And so, everything associated with the universal energy that rules the universe is positive and allows higher levels of creation and expansion associated with other correlated realities, being the dreams of other beings and other parallel realities in which the consciousness can manifest itself. Along this path, the negative will be everything that prevents this creation and ascension. This is why, "for some truth is an insult, and for others the life of the dead" (Gary Amirault).

Anyone who opposes the truth is, let it be said, bad by nature. All people with demonic tendencies, or psychopaths, if we can differentiate both, tend to base their behavior and thoughts on the art of deceiving others. At the same time, given that life is made up of creation, what prevents creation, leads to destruction and death.

Curiously, people of lies tend to oppose not only the social system as a whole but also creative projects, except when they benefit their personal ambitions. Nevertheless, evil is intrinsic to everything that composes the material universe in which we are inserted and will be manifest whenever this universe does not follow a cyclical process of permanent construction and transformation.

We can say that what follows the positive path never destroys because it transforms. Destruction itself forces transformation. And yet, destruction causes a transformation by change and not through complementarity.

This dance of forces is always proportional to each other, none of which can truly annul the other, except at the level of the mode with which we perceive them. The difference is that in a positive learning a being learns more about himself, he transforms his personality, and in the evolution of consciousness he makes new decisions that direct his life towards a different path where he finds greater peace and happiness.

The being that is forced to learn in a negative context learns about himself in a context of differentiation and comparison, and will see, in change, a forced transformation, in which it destroys a cycle to create another more suited to his existential needs.

Although the positive and the negative can be confused on the same plane of reality, they are different from each other, especially if analyzed in an extremely superficial way, in the causes and ends they seek to achieve. Because the negative forces change and creates change through re-creation, positive leads to awareness and creates change by transformation. And although we can affirm that evil can give rise to good, by destroying that evil to give place to good, we can't say that evil causes good directly. Likewise, good can transform reality, but in increasing his errors, a being can do more harm than good in his new reality. This does not mean, however, that good has created evil. Reality is in constant transformation and change, both through awareness and destruction, but in this process it is up to us to discern the way through the effects of our actions over our reality, and, nonetheless, also on ourselves.

While reality can only function by following positive assumptions associated between one another, evil, as a manifestation of error in the process, will be present throughout this learning course. For it would not make sense a learning in which error was not included. If so, we could not call it learning. It is in free will that a being becomes aware of the importance of self.

On a higher plane, the being understands that there is no good or evil, but simply dynamics that tend to follow in different directions. Before this consciousness, the being learns, for example, to destroy efficiently to create something good, like a sculptor who makes a formless stone into a beautiful sculpture.

The Illusion of Spiritual Immunity

Evil can't be avoided, but only confronted, because it consists of an energy over which we do not have decision-making power, but only control over its impact through our reactions. Evil enters into a dynamic energy that prevents the association of something positive and the continuity of a beneficial process. Thus, it cannot prevent the good in itself, unless it can capture the attention and emotions of the individual. Hence it is difficult to say without complexity that only evil prevents good actions and positive results.

These energies can easily be identified in toxic relationships, in which, regardless of appearances, we can clearly see one partner supporting the other in the decisions, while the other partner insists on preventing the former with insults, and criticisms as well as promises and agreements which are never fulfilled. To the extent that a human being has the potential to dream, as long as he dreams not even a prison of physical character can stop him. However, the power of evil is relative to the power that is attributed to it. And this can be verified from both a positive and a negative perspective.

In an analysis of the consequences, it turns out that evil becomes difficult to resist simply because it withdraws its strength from our weaknesses, even though these are physical or dependent on critical moments in our lives. How many people did not withstand a moment of weakness during a period of financial hardship, and robbed the very company where they worked? And how many more have not gotten involved with psychopaths and criminals because of a sexual attraction or attraction to financial assets held by such individuals? And how many people did not kill during a time of excesses, with drugs or alcohol, only to later realize something they would regret forever?

I believe that evil is very often dismissed and devalued by people as arrogant as they are stupid, who understand nothing about life. Many of these, ironically, easily identified in religious groups. For there is nothing better for evil than the false sense of immunity.

A Christian who believes he is protected from evil just because he meets with his group every week is like promiscuous people who have sex with strangers but think they are immune to sexual diseases simply because they know such strangers in normal contexts of socialization, such as clubs and bars.

Many of the most horrible people I met in my life were Christians and psychologists. For these are the ones who tend to assume a more preponderant illusory arrogance, often fed by society, which precisely sees in them a kind of social and spiritual immunity.

I would say that to believe that a psychologist, a psychiatrist, and a Christian, are immune to demonic effects, neurosis, or psychopathy, may be comparable to Egyptian and Greek, or even Hindu myths that identify some special people as immortal. The same has happened to those who feel immune to crime. What disillusionment these individuals must have felt when they realized they could be poisoned, pierced by a sword or arrow, or possessed by demonic spirits.

Just as many kings and gurus considered themselves immortal, and died in agony, many priests were and still are possessed by demonic spirits. And although Jesus never denied his mortality, Mohammed could more easily be compared to modern Christians, for not even after being poisoned did he believe that he would die, and not be saved by God.

The stupidest comment I ever heard from a Christian was, "God does not punish." For such a comment represents arrogance taken to the extreme. And I am not surprised that such a person is a member of the Jehovah's Witnesses, for they, like Evangelicals, demonstrate such arrogance that it can only be concealed by an equivalent kind of ignorance; such an ignorance, which completely disregards many clear passages of their own bible.

It is too incredible to be observed, but the truth is that the vast majority of religious individuals completely deny obvious contradictions in their practices vis-à-vis what their books present, and ardently advocate their own ignorance, demonstrating that excesses in egocentrism can't be overcome even with the best intentions or greater truths.

The Path of the Chosen by God

No evil is strong enough to stop the good, but it can cause good to prevent itself, because before a state of emotional pain, psychological suffering and intense worry, the individual ceases to dream and all other procedures who operate in his favor and in the pursuit of happiness. Therefore, it is not so much about what evil can prevent, but about the potential it holds in restraining the human being for whom it is intended.

One can therefore say that only courage overcomes evil. For it is the confrontation that forces the individual to take responsibility for the evil that has crossed his personal reality. But can courage be trained? The answer is yes, but within certain limits, namely physical ones. It is difficult to train courage emotionally without a life experience that balances inner capacity with external challenges, and that is why the number of suicides among many seemingly strong and psychologically healthy men is far superior to that of women. Yet evil, or suffering in general, never survives in a dynamic parallel to good, but rather interspersed with good.

The being who makes more efforts to transform the reality that surrounds him will be subject to a greater level of evil on the part of all those who fear these transformations. Higher-level beings will always be confronted with lower-level beings. But those who are at medium levels can interact with all without being included in the scope of any, such is the main stratum of society, in which the vast majority commit evil for lack of participation and intervention when their conscience so obliges. This is what happens when children who are bullied are ignored by teachers and colleagues. This is what happens when a person passes out on the street, and other people refuse to assist or call an ambulance. And, in general, this is what happens when the majority submits to tyrannical governments. Therefore, the majority of society is easily manipulated but also quite susceptible to the need for happiness, which allows this manipulation more easily, namely through fear.

The ability to make compromises with our values, and which involve walking a certain way of life, despite all the difficulties that may include, is intrinsically related to responsibility. Therefore, the individual will be all the more courageous, and hence more capable of fighting evil, the more responsibility he is able to acquire and accept. Whoever can confront evil with courage, has the responsibility to eliminate such evil and will take possession of it in order to know enough about his surrounding reality for the achievement of that goal.

On the other hand, we know that fear is the main source of energy of everything that aspires to the demonic. In fear, it is possible to stop the ability to act or even to dream. Fear, however, does not have to be directly associated with an act. Often it is the fear of losing something that leads to crime. In several experiments on morality, it is asked: "Would you kill to save a life?"; and "steal someone to save a life?" The vast majority of people responded that yes and justified this act with a moral attitude towards human life. And yet such justification of the immoral act is precisely what lies behind criminal acts. Even the thief who steals money believes he is only swinging a social injustice practiced against him. And in this sense, we could say that, at the moral level of those who commit the crime, everyone would be immune from guilt. It is the perspective of social justice that leads us to judge crime as such. That is, the higher the moral state of a society, the more many acts considered normal are seen as criminal acts. Hence a society never has a moral level superior to that of its rulers.

The Perception of Justice and the Spiritual Levels

We can't fail to see evil as a prospect subject to statistical relativity. For all drugs whose use becomes widespread, easily become lawful. Every generalized sex act becomes lawful. And any generalized criminal act becomes legal as well. It is naive of this same social majority, to think that the laws were created to prevent them from committing crimes. Laws, such as negative school classifications, and any other social evaluation and control mechanism, are always applied to a minority.

There must be a certain balance between justice and fear, and this is easily recognized by many governments. For fear stops movement; and yet because everything in the universe is in permanent motion, the only movement that ceases with fear is that which promotes exteriorization and creativity; so that with fear, an intrinsic movement takes place, which calls into question the whole identity of being. All governments that use fear as a weapon of social control, seek to keep it within certain limits, in order to maintain power without losing control in the process. The loss of such balance has drastic consequences, as we have seen in many oppressed populations who eventually rebel. It was in this way that the Soviet Union came to an end, though it was a very well-crafted Machiavellian weapon.

Those who surrender to fear lose the ability to possess self-love and to act on their conscientiousness. They will be as an automata before social premises and surrender to the immediate pleasures, because they will not know how to reach greater awareness of themselves in a long-term divine journey. They are easily governed by their governments, but also by unscrupulous dictators and rebels. Fear is the mother of chaos. Whenever a society is subject to fear, that society is susceptible to luck and superstition. A population subject to fear loses the potential to attain happiness and finds it not even with its liberation from those oppressing it. And it is for this reason that evil always tries to install fear in a first approach. For a human being cannot be prevented from acting or transforming, without first preventing him from dreaming. Fear is the only emotion that can prevent the hope that the dream feeds. And without dreams, any project, including projects aimed at liberating civilizations, are bound to fail.

With the independence of the Soviet Union, people from countries such as Latvia, Lithuania and Estonia believed themselves to be on the path to happiness, yet they faced their darkest years. Today, these people, after facing a decade of extreme poverty and hunger, continue to be victims of their fears, because they retain the highest level of suicide and distrust among citizens.

Can we then say that fear makes people evil? Not necessarily! It is hard to say that there are bad people without first talking about conscience of evil. In this sense, we can say that there are consciously bad people and unconsciously bad people. And both the former and the latter practice evil. The difference between the first and the second is almost indescribable, for while the practitioner deliberately does it because he enjoys it, others do so because they identify with that feeling and see in that evil the only way to achieve a personal good. We might even say that selfishness and fear make evil seen as necessary. And so, "the truth is hate speech only to those who have something to hide" (Michael Rivero).

In both cases, we could say that they are human beings deluded by ignorance. For to think that evil is good is an idea created through negative life experiences, where learning about the purpose of existence was formed on wrong premises, however assimilated through suffering, and a lack of morality, practically sociopath or psychopath, which derives from this same experience.

In a pragmatic perspective on life, it could be said that evil always wins. However, it is not possible to be evil and to attack the order of the cosmos simultaneously, without suffering consequences — spiritual and mental. Therefore, all persons who practice evil act against themselves, because they create such a deterioration, which occurs first at the level of consciousness.

How Negative Actions Affect Consciousness

Evil diminishes the potential of consciousness because it forces the individual to face painful situations, resulting from his behaviors, words and decisions, which he wishes to avoid. And this is where we find the main cause of psychopathy, because we are not so much victims of the circumstances as we are of our way of acting on them. And a psychopath is someone who for many years of his life has developed a huge set of neurological interconnections in the sense of becoming effective and comfortable with lying, manipulation, and deception, regardless of the emotional or even physical implications in others. Thus, all who practice evil, are trapped in an increasingly complex web of pain, which, however, they have become accustomed to. Most of these implications are social, and yet psychopaths are accustomed to being alone or living with individualism.

The solitude problem that exists in today's world is not so much a social problem, or derived from the implications of the use of new technologies, as it is a generalized mental problem, in which the vast majority of people simply do not know how to include empathy in communication, or feel responsibility for their actions, something that cannot be avoided without serious consequences. Suffice is to think that in the earliest times, being alone was practically a death sentence in an extremely hostile world.

Today, on the contrary, the pleasure of hurting others is derived from competitive motivations, a pleasure from pain for pain, which is accepted as necessary and commonplace. And this translates into a form of chronic masochism, a kind of pleasure in living from the fiery fire of such hell, maintained by resentment, envy, and hatred. Many of these people identify with this existential state and suffer in the ignorance that there are other existential universes to which they can belong by the mere decision of their will.

What is interesting about evil is that even the being who acts negatively seeks, like the one who acts positively, the awareness of self and existence; people who practice evil feel more alive in this dynamic, and believe that they can learn more about existence in this cycle of behavior; it is the attempt to awaken from a deep sleep, from the awakening of the sleeping consciousness, reason why many gurus believe that all paths, with a greater or lesser degree of evolution, eventually lead to the same positive result, to the same God.

In this sense, evil people are beings of sleeping consciousness and are disconnected from their spirit, without a soul at work, heading for oblivion. In fact, all manifestations that signal this, such as nightmares at night, and depression during the day, tend to be overlooked with excess alcohol, drugs and other risky behaviors. In this existential emptiness, they do not recognize any meaning in their existences or purpose in their lives. They do not believe in the meaning of life and live a life of no importance.

It is not a coincidence that the people who most make others suffer tend to be atheists, since generally atheists do not have a moral relationship with the world, but rather a selfish one. Although atheism has no direct relation to morality, it tends to attract the most immoral. Just as religion repels those who detest morality.

There are inherent abilities of the spirit that are materialized in the brain to allow its use, through the power of the soul, as well as in the genetic code of each of us, which changes permanently, but the development in society of contemporary ideas make it atrophy. In experiencing the material world, we can lose the reason it assumes about our spiritual evolution, and not be able to see that in all emotions, our reality assumes a purpose that intertwines with our eternal development, far beyond what the physical body will ever allow. But who knows how to listen in silence, will be able to feel in the dark and see beyond the senses. Beyond what the eyes see and the ears hear, there is a reality beyond the material world. This is the reality of feelings. In it we recognize ourselves and recognize everything else. Because in the immaterial world we find the purpose of the material world.

The opposite is also true, since material reality has as its objective to convey to the logic and purpose of the spiritual world, in our feelings, we find our way, and we will see who we should or should not associate with or who we should listen to and follow. This consciousness is best developed in the absence of reason guided by social premises or by the intellect formed by the senses of the body. It is the way of the heart.

It is not so much whether we are good or necessarily bad ourselves, but rather we create meaningful associations with which we can transform ourselves in a positive way. And so it can be said that it is better to learn to transcend the social nature of the human being when it is deeply rooted in an immoral society, and learn about it when surrounded by highly ethical people.

Someone unaware of his negative potential, can see in an individual with positive potential a source of danger, confusion and pain, confusing this person in a negative cycle. This is because between positive and negative everything that exists is antagonism. Therefore, malice is based on an assumption based on irresponsible roots and intellectual immaturity, and becomes even more serious before a greater degree of unconsciousness in what regards to the consequences of the acts of those who practice them.

Forgiveness and understanding play a very important role here, as catalysts for the dissolution of the conflict. In the resolution of antagonism lies the source of wisdom and the product of transformation. To understand who allows us to create positivity or not, we must consider the communicative and empathic potential of that person, as we will find greater understanding in who is more positive and least in whom is more negative. For understanding is the demonstration of the potential and willingness to assimilate and co-create.

The Assimilation of Sin and Divine Punishment

Given that there is an order in the universe that governs existence, sin is all the act that operates against this order, interpreted by many as sacred geometry or sacred moral order. He who acts against the cosmic order also acts against himself, because he is within the same order and is a direct effect of it. He who does something sinful will feel the weight on the level of consciousness, and karma, also feeling less mental clarity and feeling less at peace with himself. Therefore, "it is better to be divided by truth than to be united in error" (Adrian Rodgers).

As an example, we can call sins all the acts that consist of hurting others, orally or physically, or acts that violate the free will of other human beings, their freedom to choose, even though we may see that their actions are negative. Here are included acts that consist of preventing or stopping the movement of others, except when it is a negative movement against and interfering with our integrity. But also acts that seek to change a natural and positive order to give way to another negative and destructive.

Sin is the direct or indirect attack on one's own life in the action against third parties. In this sense, sin can't be defined in itself, but rather in action, because an action can only be identified as positive or negative through the context in which it is inserted. Ultimately, an act is considered positive when it promotes the greatest number of present and future elements, and negative, when it motivates their elimination. Nevertheless, there are situations where the minority element is more worthy of promotion than the majority, and in the case of humans, this is very common, for few people have moved the planet in one direction more positive and against the will of the majority of their time.

Along this line, we cannot speak of a punishing God given the fact that there is a universal order in which everything is inserted. The order in which all reality and beings are inserted is an order of energy in itself, in which the goal aims at transformation in harmony with spiritual awareness. The purpose of human life is to create in the same order, discovering it and learning, in the interaction of creative action with the product of individual action. Thus, if we have to speak in punishment, we should also refer to the feeling of spiritual emptiness that accompanies creation without love, that is, selfish action. That is, it is not so much the punishment that God can inflict, but the punishment a being inflicts on himself by actions that attempt against existence.

Considering the aforementioned, it is not relevant to speak of the action of a superior agent, inasmuch as the logic of the universe already created presupposes, a priori, the acceptance of a responsibility on all those who act in accordance with its dynamics. This dynamic logic, which acts on all earthly life and other worlds, as well as different interdimensional planes, is endowed with a unique purpose that integrates all existence, thus self-sufficient in its structures and mechanism. This is why karma is not so much about a relationship between reincarnations as it is about a relationship of the spirit with the effects of its decisions and actions.

Everything in our world has prices, punishments and rewards, long before human beings think about the meaning of these concepts. "The truth is rarely pure and never simple" (Oscar Wilde). And yet we could not have created an organized material world without first discovering the spiritual laws that regulate chaos. All that humanity has done is to bring its order, through personal and collective needs, into this chaos, uniting the visible and invisible worlds.

A The Bridge Between the Visible and the Invisible

In death we find an opportunity to get rid of the personality, which prevents consciousness from rising to higher levels. Whenever it arises, it ends with one cycle of existence to begin another. However, the resumption of existence into another physical and temporal plane gives continuity to the previous one, so that all unfinished learning will have continuity in the following life plans, and all those that have been completed will cease in these new cycles. This does not mean, however, that there is a direct relationship between the level of experience acquired, since a French monarch can easily be reborn among Portuguese peasants and feel from birth that the people around him are too ignorant, whereas they are likely to discriminate him for being too different and too educated for the context in which he is inserted. So it is with geniuses of science who are reborn in poor environments where they are not understood. On the other hand, many people also forget their competence and responsibility in changing their present future. And, despite the limits that society imposes on itself, it is possible to change country, change passport and nationality, and even change name. Cosmetic surgery has also allowed authentic miracles to many people, especially those who were not born with the most attractive appearance.

It is relatively easy to predict how our later reality will be presented, insofar as reality itself becomes present time. The vacuum of necessary learning must always be filled by later reality. Thus, a negative cycle that did not end in present time, will certainly not end with death. In other words, what led someone to suicide will continue with this person in the next life because it coincides with an unfinished learning.

All learning or fears remain with us between lives. The confusion that exists in many people who study the topic concerns the difference that they do not know between the faculties of the spirit and those of the mind. Most know only the faculties of the mind. But the mind is no more than a tool of thought and storehouse for memory.

It is in the spirit that emotions assume relevant proportions, and being reveals stimuli, ambitions and desires, or fears, which find no genetic response, but rather inter-lives. It is the spirit that explains everything that can't be explained by the mind. And that's why, quite honestly, I can't offer answers to all the people who ask me how I can do what I do. For they are looking for conclusions in my mind, and explanations in their mind. And all the questions that they pose me, because they fall into this context, are impossible to answer. My appearance does not meet expectations, my knowledge finds no correlation with my past, my intuition has never been trained in this life, and not even my age corresponds to my intellectual level. And curiously, age is one of the subjects that most confuses people, because they believe that knowledge is limited to the space-time of an existence.

Indeed, if we focus on the vast majority of people, we will not find great differences between their past and present. But if you come across the reincarnation of a guru, a Buddhist, a monarch, a knight, a king, and so many other people who have held relevant positions or great power in past lives, it is only natural that their present life is hard to comprehend, full of drastic decisions, gross changes, and radical attitudes. In fact, I believe that the most successful people in business have to have been relevant characters of the past due to the enormous degree of difficulties and panoply of relevant requirements to maintain a successful business such as persistence, discipline, and ability to overcome extremely tough emotional situations. Although all this can be trained, few are those who can overcome such training. Therefore, learning and training are as relevant as the ability to support both.

Trying to understand our limits or capabilities through past lives may not be easy without technical help and a certain attitude toward the topic, but even if we can do that, we better understand our spiritual journey through life experience. For example, although I was born in a very disadvantaged context and my parents taught me from birth to accept authority and always obey, from the age of twenty I began to notice in me, not only a lack of capacity to accept authority, especially when I regarded it as incompetent, which led me to be seen by many as undisciplined and rebellious, but also a natural ability to lead and do it well. And that's how I started my first company, after being president of many associations, where this leadership was obtained in a natural way.

Much more could be said as an example for this subject, though the most interesting thing here is to note that I have been able to find the answer to my abilities after discovering such capabilities. I was not surprised when, at the age of nearly forty, twenty years later, I discovered that I had been a monarch in one life.

How to Awaken Knowledge From Previous Lives?

My spiritual evolution and the application of the theories I have outlined in my books have helped me immensely to discover all the talents asleep in me, talents impossible to explain to the people I meet but who give me great pleasure to explore. For example, I have taught several medieval but also Japanese martial arts; I understand everything I read from the Hindu and Rosicrucian scriptures, which are complex even for the many members of these groups; and I have already won first place in many world electronic music competitions, as a producer and DJ, although I have never studied music all my life. And as far as language learning is concerned, the Chinese pronunciation is too easy for me to copy, as well as French and Scottish. Let us say that I can scare the natives of these countries by reading texts because I look like one of them, although I do not understand what I am reading. More than that, I understand their way of speaking and values. And these are all attributes acquired between-lives.

Still, I must say that the greatest benefit of such experiences has been to acquire the capacity to understand the history of mankind on a more realistic plane than that which is transmitted in the educational system. Not even the cinema comes so close to reality. And the regressions I made were so realistic, as shocking, for they allowed me to understand immensely about human nature, which I would never have known otherwise.

Among these experiences, the most relevant to me, was the realization that the French Revolution was a scheme used against the population, to withdraw the power of legitimate monarchic families for the purpose of creating a dictatorship in the country. It was, in other words, a military coup assisted and commanded by the clergy and Freemasonry. But it never had anything to do with the liberation of the people, not even poverty.

The French have paid dearly for their stupidity. And the truth is that these Frenchmen of the revolution were a dirty, disgusting, extremely ignorant, and easy to manipulate people. And the French Revolution was a terrible cruel injustice that killed many more innocent than guilty, if there ever was a few.

For the truth is that, throughout medieval Europe, the people, in general, have always been poor, having to live in lands that did not belong to them. And in this context, the monarchs were of great public utility, in organizing society in accordance with self-sustaining hierarchies, and with a direct assistance and support, just as monarchical governments do today in countries, we must say, much more prosperous than others where democracy takes over power. In general, the people have always been victims of their own stupidity, and never their revolutions, rulers or socioeconomic situation.

My later reincarnations have clearly shown this to me, for I have been far more betrayed in this life than in previous lives, and have always done something better than others, or because my popularity is a threat to those who seek to use manipulation, which serves to prove that the vast majority of people are as stupid and cowardly today as they ever were.

The only difference, I would say, is that this manipulation is now more difficult to identify, and is more diluted, among government officials, banking institutions, psychologists, psychiatrists, and the education system as a whole. And as for the latter case, I must say that most teachers are so stupid that they do not realize that they have been trained to manipulate, and do so, so unconsciously, that they cannot realize that their arrogance hides a huge lack of ability to really educate. If you want proof of this, just ask any teacher the following: How do you learn? For if you do not know how your students learn, the teaching is an antics. And if you follow this path, take advantage and also ask a psychiatrist, or psychologist, what mental health is. For if they can't explain well, they prove the same.

The truth is that no one is curing mental illnesses because there is not even an understanding of what this is. And no one is actually teaching because there is no understanding of how humans process information. There are many theories about everything, of course, but these theories are based on falsehoods. And it will be necessary that one day we come into contact with much more advanced extraterrestrial civilizations so that this illusion fades from the world, although many can commit suicide in the process, for not being able to deal with the fact that all their existence has been a great lie and has been the same illusion for many reincarnations.

The Transmutation of the Identity

Death does not assume negative aspects in itself, nor does it deal with interruptions, but rather with a liberation, which allows the formation of a more adequate later reality than the present. No one is punished in the next life, but all will live a life more adequate to the level of the consciousness thus acquired. Suffering often has the goal of alerting us to a life that is not being lived by the spirit and that is empty of meanings. Soon, in the next life, the being will live a reality that forces even more the search for the meaning of his existence, which means to live even more pressure in order to find it. For reality to fit the spirituality of the being, he will always find the world which is more suited to itself, as well as the more propitious context between the dynamics that govern the existential harmony in the universe. We can reincarnate in another time period or in another dimensional reality, or even in another world. But what we live today is what we will have tomorrow. We must therefore pay attention to the unfinished cycles of our existence — our worries, anxiety, desires, unreached dreams, etc.

In fact, these emotional states are behind virtually all physical and mental illnesses, so they are relatively easy to recognize. The regrets, with which many people live, make them frustrated, unhappy, and, ultimately, sick, shortening the years of life. The more peace within yourself is being found, the more certain you may be to have found your spiritual path and a better reincarnation. It is not so much about what death can change, but rather on what life can change. For death exists only for the personality and not for the spirit. Except for rare cases of famous people, social identity ends with death, but the consciousness that this identity has incorporated and developed, in its social experiences and in tune with the material world, remains with the spirit beyond the death of the body. Everything that could not be transformed in the present will have an opportunity for it, if it is relevant to the individual, in a future time, in another life.

It becomes obvious, therefore, when we look around, that the world has become much easier for scientists, painters, musicians, sculptors, writers, and other individuals who wish to express their spiritual and creative potential, notwithstanding the difficulties they still support during their journey on the planet. More than this, the more we can resolve in our present life regarding our karma, the less burden we will bring with us for the next lives.

"We are not generally prepared for the truth, which is why it is revealed to us progressively" (Chip Brogden). But, everything is possible, in life and death. There is nothing that can't be solved in any way in our present life or after it. Everything has a solution, although this does not coincide with our concept of solving a problem. Whenever a problem disappears from our consciousness, we can say that it is solved regardless of how it happened. Therefore, it is in consciousness that we find the formula to best solve our life.

Sometimes, following the consciousness, we can transform our present life so much that we will feel to be living different personalities. It is the sensation of ceasing to be who we were to live in the skin of a new person. Whenever this happens, it means that we have succeeded in transforming our life, and we must continue this path in order to achieve the maximum happiness possible.

The more we follow the voice of our consciousness, the more we will transform our present reality. And these transformations will be so significant that it will seem that we die to be reborn in the body of a new individual.

Life goes faster for those who are in tune with the divine energy and found God's purpose in their personal happiness. For these people, life is a world of opportunities in the path of happiness. And for them, death will play a derisory role, since for those who live life in full, death will be less feared, since it is not so unknown.

This person has already lived the death of himself, in present time, whenever he abdicated what he appears to the others for the sake of his personal happiness. This is what many explain as the death of the ego, although it is this and more. It is an alchemical process of inner transformation, at all levels, i.e., intellectual, emotional, spiritual and even sexual. Sexual energy, being primordially of biological origin, represents one of the states more difficult to transform, but also the most relevant to evaluate our transition of personality.

YOUR SOUL PURPOSE

Inner truth is always superior to any interpretation or reason external to the subject. But there is no morality that assumes more reason than personal ethics, and that is why oppressive governments will always be destroyed by the unscrupulous population which they originated. For this reason, and because a large part of the population is at extremely low levels of humanism and conscience, we are often obliged to make sacrifices, in order to reach higher levels of happiness, in which we include the whole image of who we are, and the possibility of gaining a bad reputation. This implies giving up pride, property, friends and material security for the sake of dreams. All the transformations demand these exchange coins, and those who have emigrated for better living conditions know them well. Only to the most courageous and daring in the path of happiness belongs the destiny of God, although it is engraved in the spirit of all human beings.

It is harder to be unhappy than happy. Only the illusion created by most people who think otherwise leads us to think that it is not so. Just try to ignore a problem and notice how others react to it, even when the problem does not belong to them, to realize this. In the world we live in, those who do not watch the news and do not read newspapers are always seen as a social misfit, ignoramus or even a madman. These people are unaware that it is more important to spend a day observing a beautiful flower and sunbathing than looking at a box full of stories of terror and war. So we can't solve the vast majority of our problems, but learning to ignore them is truly an art.

About the Publisher

This book was published by the 22 Lions Bookstore.
For more books like this visit www.22Lions.com.
Join us on social media at:
Fb.com/22Lions;
Twitter.com/22lionsbookshop;
Instagram.com/22lionsbookshop;
Pinterest.com/22LionsBookshop.

www.ingramcontent.com/pod-product-compliance
Lightning Source LLC
Chambersburg PA
CBHW050446010526
44118CB00013B/1710